DEC - - 2014

2/16(1)

Ripley's Believe It or Not!®

Developed and produced by Ripley Publishing Ltd

This edition published and distributed by:

Mason Crest
450 Parkway Drive, Suite D, Broomall, PA 19008
www.masoncrest.com

Printed and bound in the United States of America

First printing
9 8 7 6 5 4 3 2 1

Ripley's Believe It or Not!
Amazing Feats
ISBN: 978-1-4222-3139-5 (hardback)
Ripley's Believe It or Not!—Complete 8 Title Series
ISBN: 978-1-4222-3138-8

Cataloging-in-Publication Data is on file with the Library of Congress

PUBLISHER'S NOTE
While every effort has been made to verify the accuracy of the entries in this book, the
Publishers cannot be held responsible for any errors contained in the work. They would
be glad to receive any information from readers.

WARNING
Some of the stunts and activities in this book are undertaken by experts and should not
be attempted by anyone without adequate training and supervision.

Ripley's Believe It or Not!®

Dare To Look

AMAZING FEATS

www.MasonCrest.com

AMAZING FEATS

Extraordinary exploits. Read about

the most astounding achievements.

Meet the brave volcano chaser,

the professional camel jumpers,

and the man who skydived from

the edge of space to Earth!

Anthony Martin escaped from this locked
casket while falling through the air at
130 mph (210 km/h)...

VOLCANO CHASER

Photographer and thrill-seeker Geoff Mackley stood on a spot where no human has ever been before—just 100 ft (30 m) above a boiling lake of 2,100°F (1,150°C) lava in an active volcano. Even though he was wearing a special fire suit and breathing apparatus, just one slip or a sudden surge of the bubbling lava would have turned him instantly to ash.

Geoff, from Christchurch, New Zealand, specializes in photographing spectacular natural phenomena, including hurricanes, cyclones, and tornadoes, but this ultimate quest to reach the Marum Volcano on one of the Pacific islands of Vanuatu, 1,200 mi (1,900 km) off the northeast coast of Australia, took him 15 years of planning.

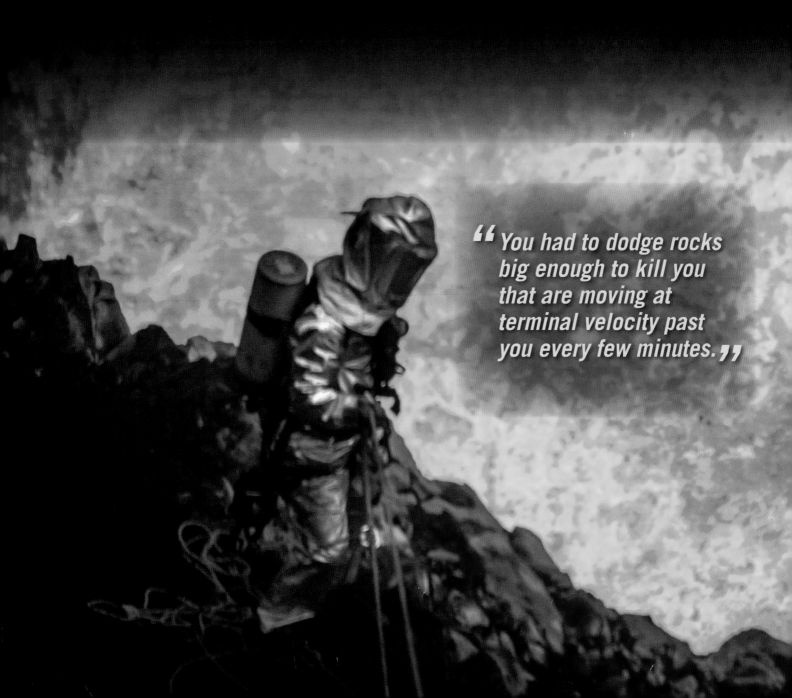

"You had to dodge rocks big enough to kill you that are moving at terminal velocity past you every few minutes."

On his first day, Geoff climbed down toward the volcano. When he reached the rim he stood without his protective suit, but the heat was so intense that he had to cover his face and run back after just six seconds. All too aware that over 200,000 people have died from volcanic eruptions in the past five centuries, he knew that just one gulp of the superheated air coming off the lava would kill him instantly.

With its lava lake the size of 2½ football fields, the Marum Volacno emits heat that is as fierce as that from the flame of a blowtorch, nearly five times hotter than the maximum temperature of a conventional oven, and more than 20 times hotter than the record temperature at Death Valley, California. A volcano's lava tubes are so efficient in containing heat that lava flowing as far as 6 mi (9.6 km) from the center of a volcano cools only by about 18°F (10°C).

Just to reach the edge of the lava pit, Geoff had to climb down a 1,200-ft (366-m) vertical drop—that's almost the height of New York City's Empire State Building. He donned the suit and breathing apparatus and descended again to create history by standing next to the volcano for 40 minutes. He was so focused on what lay before him that his colleagues eventually had to warn him that he was running out of air in his breathing gear.

CHURCH LICKER

▶ To win a bet with a friend, Lawrence Edmonds of London has licked all 42 of England's Anglican cathedrals. His 17-month, 5,000-mi (8,000-km) tour saw him place his tongue on the stonework of cathedrals that included Durham, York, Canterbury, and Winchester.

JUMP FLIP▶ Hollywood stuntman Robert Souris set a record-breaking longest forward jump flip when he achieved a leap of 19 ft 11½ in (6.08 m) at Davie, Florida, on July 4, 2012. He celebrated by doing four backflips.

BALLOON FLOWERS▶ Ralf Esslinger, Thomas Hinte, and Guido Verhoef created 2,335 balloon flowers in eight hours on May 13, 2012, at a garden show in Nagold, Germany. Each flower consisted of at least two balloons.

BOTTLE CAPS▶ Pupils at Ambrosoli International School in Bugolobi, Uganda, strung 34,149 bottle caps into one continuous chain measuring 508 ft (155 m) long.

PAPER PLANE▶ On February 26, 2012, former football quarterback Joe Ayoob threw a paper airplane a world-record distance of 226 ft 10 in (69.1 m) inside a hangar at McClellan Air Force Base near Sacramento, California. Built by John Collins, who has designed real airplanes for many years, the paper missile was made from A4 paper and a small piece of sticky tape.

YOUNGEST COWBOY▶ Aged just 2½, Royce Gill from New South Wales is a regular on the Australian rodeo circuit, riding against cowboys more than seven times his age. Royce, the world's youngest rodeo star, rides a six-year-old miniature pony called Maybelline and is the seventh-generation rodeo rider in his family.

MARATHON RIDE▶ Californian Gus Martinez rode for 25 hours, with just a five-minute break each hour, aboard the 130-ft-tall (40-m) Ferris wheel at Santa Monica Pier's Pacific Park—even though he doesn't like heights.

FLYING HIGH

▶ On July 28, 2011, children in Gaza, Palestine, flew a record number of 12,350 kites simultaneously along a 1.2-mile (1.9-km) stretch of beach in an event organized by the United Nations Relief and Works Agency. It was the seventh world record that children from Gaza had broken in two years.

BIONIC WOMAN▶ 32-year-old Claire Lomas from Leicestershire, England, who was left paralyzed from the chest down following a horseback-riding accident in 2007, became the first person to complete a marathon in a bionic suit when she finished the 2012 London Marathon in 16 days. Hundreds of people lined the streets as she made her final steps to cross the line.

OLDEST SHOPKEEPER▶ After 78 years of standing behind the counter of his haberdashery store at Greater Manchester, England, Britain's oldest shopkeeper, Jack Yaffe, finally retired in 2012 at age 103.

LIFT OFF▶ At the 2011 Albuquerque International Balloon Festival, a world record 345 hot-air balloons were launched in a single hour.

PERIODIC TABLE▶ Scientists at the Nanotechnology and Nanoscience Centre from the University of Nottingham, England, used an electron microscope and an ion beam writer to carve the periodic table of elements onto a single strand of hair—belonging to chemistry professor Martyn Poliakoff. The world's smallest periodic table, measuring just 89.67 by 46.39 microns, it is so tiny that a million copies of it would fit on a standard-sized Post-it note.

SHOULDER STRENGTH

▶ A stuntman in Nanning, China, demonstrates his incredible shoulder blade muscles by using them to pull a cart containing ten women and by gripping an iron between them (below).

EGG BALANCING▶ A total of 4,247 eggs were stood upright simultaneously on individual tiles during the 2012 Dragon Boat Festival in Hsinchu City, Taiwan. The tradition of balancing eggs at noon on the day of the festival supposedly guarantees a year of good luck.

NAKED ROWERS▶ In January 2012, the British quintet of Debbie Beadle, Julia Immonen, Katie Pattison-Hart, Kate Richardson, and Helen Leigh rowed across the Atlantic Ocean in a record 45 days and, to avoid friction burns from clothing, they made most of the trip naked. Their 2,600-mi (4,184-km) crossing took them from the Canary Islands to Barbados—the first all-female crew to complete the voyage.

VERTICAL DIVE▶ A total of 138 skydivers broke the world record for vertical skydiving—beating the previous best by 30—when they flew headfirst in a snowflake formation over Ottawa, Illinois, falling at speeds of up to 220 mph (354 km/h).

QR MAZE▶ The Kraay family designed a huge, 312,000-sq-ft (29,000-sq-m) corn maze on their farm near Lacombe, Alberta, Canada, to operate as a fully functioning QR (Quick Response) code. When scanned from the skies—the test flight went as high as 14,000 ft (4,260 m)—with a smartphone, the code sent the user to the website for the Kraay Family Farm. The Kraay family have been carving corn mazes into their crops for more than 13 years.

WHEELCHAIR JUMP▶ Paraplegic bungee jumper Christine Rougoor plunged 150 ft (46 m) from a bridge into a ravine at Whistler, Canada, while in a wheelchair. The chair actually provided more stability for the bungee jump, stopping blood from rolling around her body too fast and preventing blackouts.

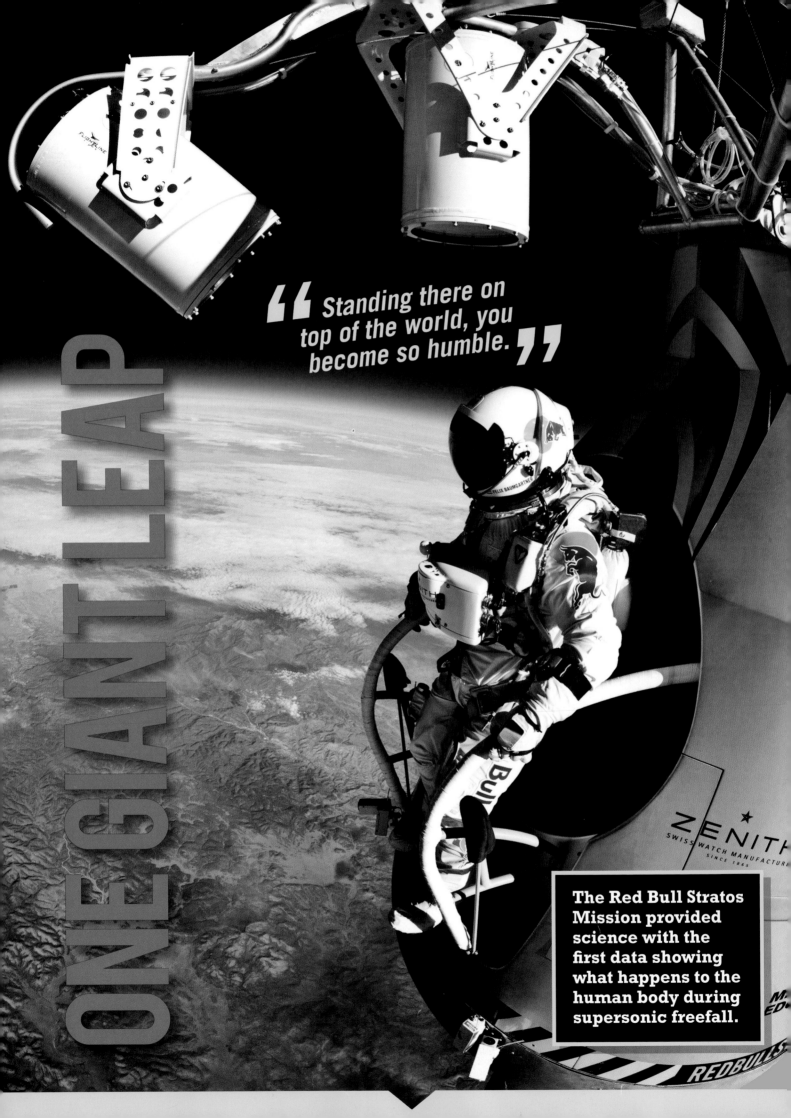

ONE GIANT LEAP

" Standing there on top of the world, you become so humble. "

The Red Bull Stratos Mission provided science with the first data showing what happens to the human body during supersonic freefall.

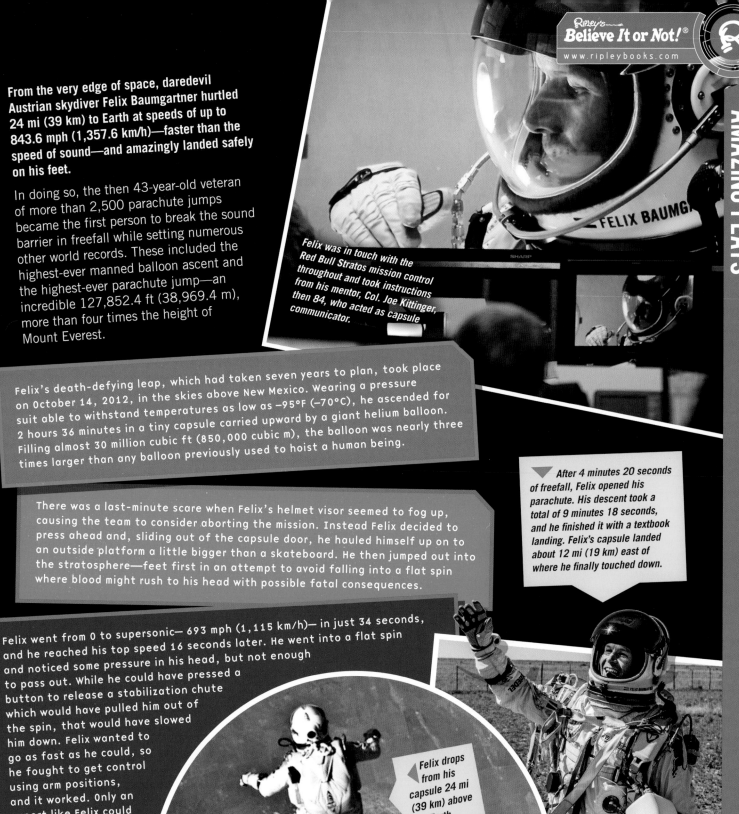

Ripley's
Believe It or Not!®
www.ripleybooks.com

From the very edge of space, daredevil Austrian skydiver Felix Baumgartner hurtled 24 mi (39 km) to Earth at speeds of up to 843.6 mph (1,357.6 km/h)—faster than the speed of sound—and amazingly landed safely on his feet.

In doing so, the then 43-year-old veteran of more than 2,500 parachute jumps became the first person to break the sound barrier in freefall while setting numerous other world records. These included the highest-ever manned balloon ascent and the highest-ever parachute jump—an incredible 127,852.4 ft (38,969.4 m), more than four times the height of Mount Everest.

Felix was in touch with the Red Bull Stratos mission control throughout and took instructions from his mentor, Col. Joe Kittinger, then 84, who acted as capsule communicator.

Felix's death-defying leap, which had taken seven years to plan, took place on October 14, 2012, in the skies above New Mexico. Wearing a pressure suit able to withstand temperatures as low as –95°F (–70°C), he ascended for 2 hours 36 minutes in a tiny capsule carried upward by a giant helium balloon. Filling almost 30 million cubic ft (850,000 cubic m), the balloon was nearly three times larger than any balloon previously used to hoist a human being.

There was a last-minute scare when Felix's helmet visor seemed to fog up, causing the team to consider aborting the mission. Instead Felix decided to press ahead and, sliding out of the capsule door, he hauled himself up on to an outside platform a little bigger than a skateboard. He then jumped out into the stratosphere—feet first in an attempt to avoid falling into a flat spin where blood might rush to his head with possible fatal consequences.

After 4 minutes 20 seconds of freefall, Felix opened his parachute. His descent took a total of 9 minutes 18 seconds, and he finished it with a textbook landing. Felix's capsule landed about 12 mi (19 km) east of where he finally touched down.

Felix went from 0 to supersonic— 693 mph (1,115 km/h)— in just 34 seconds, and he reached his top speed 16 seconds later. He went into a flat spin and noticed some pressure in his head, but not enough to pass out. While he could have pressed a button to release a stabilization chute which would have pulled him out of the spin, that would have slowed him down. Felix wanted to go as fast as he could, so he fought to get control using arm positions, and it worked. Only an expert like Felix could stop such a spin using skydiving skills alone.

Felix drops from his capsule 24 mi (39 km) above the Earth.

ALTITUDE COMPARISON

■ Mount Everest	29,029 ft (8,848 m)
■ Jet airplane cruising	35,000 ft (10,700 m)
■ Concorde cruising	56,000 ft (17,000 m)
■ Felix Baumgartner	127,852.4 ft (38,969.4 m)

FIELD GOALS▶ On October 9, 2011, Craig Pinto of Mineola, New York State, kicked a record 1,000 regulation 40-yard (36.5-m) American Football field goals in 24 hours.

SAMOAN JOY▶ American Samoa were the joint-lowest-ranked national soccer team in the world when they won their first-ever international match, beating Tonga 2–1 in a World Cup qualifier in November 2011. With a population of just 55,000, the U.S. protectorate had lost every competitive game they had played in more than 17 years, including a 31–0 mauling by Australia in 2001.

HOCKEY MARATHON▶ In May 2012, a hockey game at Chestermere, Alberta, Canada, lasted an epic 246 hours—that's more than ten days—making it the longest hockey game ever.

MEN BANNED▶ When fans of teams from the Turkish Soccer Association get excessively rowdy, adult men are temporarily banned and only women and children are permitted to attend the games.

KITEBOARDING RECORD▶ Setting off from Whale Harbor, Islamorada, Florida, in February 2012, Lithuanian-born Rimas Kinka kiteboarded an astonishing distance of 401 mi (645 km) in just 24 hours.

MAKESHIFT SHOES▶ When he was younger, Kenyan athlete David Rudisha, who won gold at the 2012 Olympics when he ran the fastest-ever 800 meters, would cut up used car tires to serve as makeshift running shoes.

KING KAYAK
▶ At a little over 407 ft (124 m) long, this enormous kayak can seat 100 people! Built to mark the centenary of outdoor retailer L.L. Bean, the king-sized craft—made up of 100 standard kayaks—took its maiden voyage at Freeport, Maine, in June 2012.

PLAYING IN THE LAKE▶ In the drought-hit area around Imotski, Croatia, in November 2011, two local soccer teams were able to play on the dry bed of a lake that normally contains millions of gallons of reservoir water. The makeshift soccer field was carved out of the dust at Modro Jezero (The Blue Lake), which is usually as much as 500 ft (150 m) underwater.

FIRST 1080▶ At Tehachapi, California, on March 30, 2012, 12-year-old Tom Schaar from Malibu nailed the first-ever 1,080-degree skateboard turn by making three complete revolutions in midair before landing. Tom, who has been skateboarding since the age of four, achieved the historic feat on the 70-ft-tall (21.3-m) MegaRamp, which launches skaters up to 15 ft (4.5 m) in the air.

LUCKY SOCKS▶ At the London 2012 Olympics, veteran Great Britain rower Greg Searle wore the same pair of lucky socks that he had worn when winning gold at the 1992 Barcelona Olympics, making the socks older than four of his 2012 team-mates!

FAMILY PUNISHMENT▶ For touching a gate in the qualifying round of the men's kayak competition at the 2012 London Olympics, New Zealand's Mike Dawson was handed a two-second penalty by his mother, Kay, who was a judge at the Games.

BLIND ARCHER▶ South Korean archer Im Dong-hyun is a world record holder in his sport despite being legally blind, with only ten percent vision in his left eye and 20 percent in his right eye. When he looks at the targets, he sees colors with blurred lines between them.

FOOD BALL▶ Yubi lapki, an ancient seven-a-side rugby-like game played in Manipur, India, uses a coconut as a ball. Before the start of the game, the players rub their bodies with mustard oil and water so that they are difficult to tackle.

SENIOR TRIATHLETE▶ In June 2012, Arthur Gilbert of Somerset, England, completed his 41st triathlon—at age 91. The grandfather did a 550-yd (500-m) swim, followed by a 12½-mi (20-km) bicycle ride, and a 3-mi (5-km) run, finishing in 2 hours 47 minutes 22 seconds. His rigorous training regime includes going to the gym twice a week, cycling 25 mi (40 km) every Sunday, and swimming 50 lengths of his local pool every morning.

HIGH HUMP
▶ Renowned for their speed, strength, and courage, members of the Zaranique tribe in Yemen are the world's only professional camel jumpers. From a running start, jumpers attempt to clear as many camels as possible in a single leap. This champion, Bhaydar Muhammed Kubaisi, is sailing over three animals. Dating back 2,000 years, the sport is unique to the Tehama region of the country where tribesmen train all year round for competitions.

GOAL-KICKING ROBOT▶ A robot called Robo Dan proved itself as accomplished a goal-kicker as former New Zealand international rugby star Andrew Mehrtens, who scored 967 career points for the All Blacks between 1995 and 2004. The robot, built by Massey University Albany, matched Mehrtens' score of 11 successful kicks out of 12 in a special challenge.

BULL CHAMP▶ In more than two years, no U.S. rodeo rider managed to ride Bushwacker the bull for eight seconds—the minimum amount of time required to earn any points. During that period, the average time that professional riders managed to stay on the 1,600-lb (726-kg) beast was just 3.06 seconds.

CAPTAIN CANADA▶ In 2012, 65-year-old Canadian show-jumper Ian Millar—nicknamed Captain Canada—became the first person to compete in ten Olympics, having participated in the equestrian competition at every Games since 1972, except for the 1980 Moscow Olympics that Canada boycotted.

PLAIN NUTS▶ The beach volleyball competition at the 2012 Summer Olympics was disrupted because squirrels kept burying nuts and acorns on the sandy practice courts at London's St. James's Park.

▶ French Jet Ski champion Franky Zapata demonstrates his invention, the Flyboard, a motorized device that allows him to fly up to 50 ft (15 m) in the air like Superman or to dive head first through the water like a dolphin. It is powered by a Jet Ski motor that generates a water jet connected via a long hose to a pair of jet boots and handheld stabilizers.

DOLPHIN JETPACK

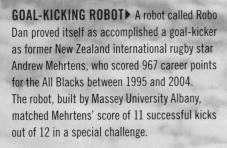

BLIND LINGUIST▶ At the age of ten, Alexia Sloane, a blind schoolgirl from Cambridge, England, who is fluent in four languages, became the youngest interpreter to work at the European Parliament. Alexia, who lost her sight when she was two after being diagnosed with a brain tumor, can speak English, French, Spanish, and Mandarin, and is learning German. She has been tri-lingual since she learned to talk, as her mother is half French and half Spanish and her father is English.

WIRE WALK▶ In August 2011, Chinese acrobat Saimaiti Aishan walked 50 ft (15 m) across a thin metal wire strung between two hot-air balloons floating 100 ft (30 m) above the ground in Hunan Province.

BOLD JUMP▶ On May 23, 2012, British stuntman Gary Connery became the first person to jump out of a helicopter and land without using a parachute. Using a special wingsuit, which he has developed to help him glide through the air and dramatically reduce speed on descent, he jumped from 2,400 ft (732 m) above Oxfordshire, England. He descended at 80 mph (128 km/h) before landing on a special runway that was made up of 18,000 cardboard boxes.

PLUCKY GUY
▶ This talented street performer in Guangzhou, China, makes sure he gets himself noticed by playing the guitar and singing while standing on his head!

BUNGEE JUMP▶ Frances Gabe of Fresno, California, celebrated her 91st birthday by bungee jumping at the local fair—a tradition she began on her 82nd birthday after overcoming a serious illness.

BRIDGE JUMP▶ To celebrate Bridge Day, every year more than 400 daredevil BASE jumpers leap off the New River Gorge Bridge in Fayetteville, West Virginia, and plunge 876 ft (267 m) into the river below. The festival, which has been running since 1980, is the only time when it is legal to BASE jump off the bridge.

BIKE CLIMB▶ On January 30, 2012, Polish cyclist Krystian Herba climbed the 2,040 steps of the 68 floors of the Rose Rayhaan by Rotana Hotel, Dubai, U.A.E., in 1 hour 13 minutes 41 seconds on his bike—a record for the most steps climbed on a bicycle.

DOMINO CHAIN▶ After weeks of hand-assembling hundreds of thousands of dominoes into a series of elaborate constructions, the Sinners Domino team toppled 127,141 of them in just seven minutes in Büdingen, Germany, in August 2012.

FAST WORKER▶ Brewery worker Benjamin Pilon of Blanco, Texas, is able to open 110 bottles of beer in 60 seconds—that's nearly two bottle caps every second.

SMASHING TIME

▶ A Belarussian soldier has a solid concrete masonry block on his chest smashed by a flaming hammer as part of the annual week-long Maslenitsa celebrations in Minsk, which showcase feats of strength.

BOTTLE BALANCE▶ Seven-year-old Romanian gymnast Giuliano Stroe can perform eight push-ups while balancing his hands and feet on four glass bottles. He has been lifting weights and practicing gymnastics since the age of two.

HUMAN TOWER▶ A 150-strong Catalan performance troupe, the Castellers de Vilafranca, built the first-ever eight-level human tower, or castell, on June 20, 2012, when they gathered on the roof deck of a skyscraper on New York City's 5th Avenue.

CHAINSAW JUGGLER▶ Ian Stewart of Nova Scotia, Canada, made 94 catches while juggling three chainsaws—all with razor-sharp teeth and the motors running—at the Hants County Exhibition in 2011. He has been juggling chainsaws for more than 15 years.

HUMAN TORCH▶ In Hamburg, Germany, in 2011, Denni Duesterhoeft ran for 393 ft (120 m) while on fire! Wearing fire-resistant clothing, the stuntman completed the record-breaking run as flames raged around his body.

HELD BREATH▶ German free diver Tom Sietas held his breath underwater for a world record 22 minutes 22 seconds at Changsha, China, on May 30, 2012. His lung capacity is 20 percent larger than average for his size. When preparing for a record attempt, he does not eat for at least five hours beforehand in order to slow his metabolism. He fills his lungs with pure oxygen to help him hold his breath for an extra 10 minutes.

FOOD FIGHT▶ On December 2, 2011, a total of 473 students and adults of Eisenhower Junior High School, Taylorsville, Utah, took part in the world's largest marshmallow fight, throwing more than 140,000 marshmallows at each other.

JOGGING RECORD▶ On July 27, 2012, 20-year-old Matthew Feldman, a student at the University of Florida, broke a 23-year-old record when he jogged one mile (1.6 km) while simultaneously juggling five balls in 6 minutes 33.6 seconds.

CLEAN GETAWAY

▶ Chained and handcuffed to the roof of an SUV as it went through a car wash in Winnipeg, Manitoba, and battered from head to toe by brushes, soap, water, and hot wax, Canadian escape artist Dean Gunnarson still managed to break free from his shackles before the vehicle reached the massive blow-dryers at the end of the wash cycle.

Young people in Moscow are playing a game that is every bit as scary as Russian roulette. It is called "extreme urban climbing" and it involves scaling as high as 1,000 ft (300 m) up the sides of the city's tallest structures—without wearing any kind of safety equipment. Up to 200 "roofers," some masked to conceal their identity from the police, have taken up the daredevil pursuit just to have their picture taken above a death-defying drop.

CLIMBING

BELLY-FLOP

▶ The 16th annual Colorado College Belly Flop Contest landed with a splash at Water World, outside Denver, in July 2012, with fearless floppers hurling themselves with little grace into the water from a height of 12 ft (3.7 m) in order to make the biggest wave. The pain is not without gain, however—as well as belly-flop glory, winners took home prizes and scholarships worth $5,000, with Paul Salcido taking the overall honors.

BACKWARD RUNNER▶ Garret Doherty from Dublin, Ireland, can run a mile backward in fewer than seven minutes. The 33-year-old successfully defended his title at the 2012 U.K. Backwards Running Championships, finishing in 6 minutes 57 seconds—more than a minute ahead of his nearest rival.

CLEAR WATER▶ Hong Kong held a swimming race across its Victoria Harbor in 2011—the first swimming race there for 33 years owing to long-standing concerns about pollution.

BOXING PRIEST▶ On April 1, 2012, Anglican priest Father Dave Smith, 50, set a new world record for the most continuous boxing rounds when he completed 120 three-minute rounds at a church in Sydney, Australia. He boxed for more than six hours, during which time he took on 66 opponents.

NEW NAME▶ In September 2011, Ron Artest, a professional basketball player with the Los Angeles Lakers, legally changed his name to Metta World Peace.

RARE CARDS▶ Baseball fan Karl Kissner picked up a dirty old cardboard box in the attic of his late grandfather's house in Defiance, Ohio, and found it contained a collection of rare, 100-year-old baseball cards worth around $3 million. He discovered some 700 cards—all in excellent condition—featuring greats such as Ty Cobb, Christy Mathewson, and Connie Mack.

LONG SHOT▶ In 2010, 14-year-old archer Zak Crawford, a Robin Hood fan from Northamptonshire, England, fired an arrow nearly 1,640 ft (500 m)—the length of five soccer pitches. His feat beat the previous world record by an incredible 492 ft (150 m).

HAND CLIMB▶ In June 2012, Spencer West of Toronto, Canada, climbed the 19,308-ft-high (5,885-m) Mount Kilimanjaro in Kenya at the age of 31—on his hands. Both of his legs were amputated when he was five, but Spencer still managed to climb Africa's highest peak by propelling his torso forward, one hand after another, up the mountain for seven days.

LOSING RUN▶ Toronto Blue Jays' pitcher Joseph "Jo-Jo" Reyes started 28 consecutive games without a single win—from June 13, 2008 until May 30, 2011.

SMURF SUPPORT

▶ Fans of England's Hartlepool United soccer team found a bizarre way to show their dedication to the cause when they traveled to the last game of the 2011–2012 season dressed as Smurfs. Surreal photographs of hundreds of blue-faced supporters making the 230-mi (370-km) trip to London for the game against Charlton Athletic spread worldwide. Dressing up for the last day of the season is a 25-year tradition at the club—unfortunately the Smurf invasion of London was not enough to secure a win for the team.

SAME NAME ▶ A soccer match took place in the town of Bungay in Suffolk, England, in May 2012 where all 22 players, the referee, the linesmen, and the reserves had the surname Bungay. In addition to players who had come from the U.K., the United States, and Australia, the mascot was eight-year-old Carla Bungay and the doctor on hand to treat injuries was Dr. Elizabeth Bungay.

DOUBLE HIT ▶ During a baseball game between the New York Yankees and the Colorado Rockies on June 25, 2011, Rockies' shortstop Troy Tulowitzki managed to hit a ball twice with a single swing of his bat.

MARATHON DRIBBLE ▶ Mark Ott of Jackson, Michigan, ran the 26-mile 2010 Martian Marathon in Dearborn in 3 hours 23 minutes 42 seconds while dribbling a basketball.

ETHNIC GAMES ▶ A demonstration of traditional ethnic Yao games at Nanning, China, included tossing a ball of fire into an opponent's basket, running across burning logs to hurl fruit at a 16-ft (5-m) target, and climbing a mountain of knives, where barefoot competitors scale a 23-ft-high (7-m) pole embedded with 36 razor-sharp blades.

HORSEY HEROINE ▶ Australian racehorse Black Caviar is so popular that a major Aussie Rules football match was rescheduled to avoid clashing with one of her races. When she first raced abroad, at Royal Ascot, England, in June 2012, thousands of people watched her record her 22nd straight win on a giant TV screen in Melbourne's Federation Square, even though it was nearly one o'clock in the morning.

▶▶ *IN 1946, AL COUTURE BEAT RALPH WALTON IN A BOXING MATCH IN 10.5 SECONDS— INCLUDING THE COUNT!* ◀

LONGEST GAME ▶ At O'Fallon, Missouri, in July 2012, 50 baseball players took part in a game that lasted 60 hours 11 minutes 32 seconds—the world's longest. In all, 169 innings were played and 451 runs scored over three afternoons with temperatures topping 100°F (38°C).

FASTEST SKATEBOARDER ▶ On June 18, 2012, Mischo Erban from Vernon, Canada, set a new world record for the fastest skateboard speed from a standing position. He clocked 80.74 mph (129.9 km/h) on a downhill run in Quebec.

CRACK CLIMBERS

▶ *A pair of determined daredevils from the U.K. traveled to Utah to become the first climbers ever to complete an infamous sheer-rock ascent. Tom Randall and Pete Whittaker squeezed themselves up Century Crack, a terrifying 120-ft (37-m) rock fissure in the Canyonlands National Park, by sliding their hands, feet, and limbs into narrow crevices only inches wide, and hauling their bodies upward. The climb is so challenging that nobody had ever completed it before. The width of the crack means that regular climbing techniques are of little use, and the men had to complete most of the ascent by hanging upside down with their feet jammed above their head. Randall and Whittaker did not take the Century Crack lightly, undergoing two years of intensive training that involved spending hours hanging from a replica of the crack in the cellar of Randall's house!*

PINNED SKIN

Kelvin Mercado from Puerto Rico smashed his way through the pain barrier to pin a new Ripley record 161 clothes pegs to his face—and he did it in the dark!

Kelvin flew to Ripley's Orlando headquarters for the attempt in 2013. With his first try he attached 173 clothespins to his face, but was disqualified because some pegs were pinned to his neck. On the second attempt he had to quit at 157 because of the pain. Finally, on his third attempt of the day, and using glow-in-the-dark pegs, he pinned 161—more than anyone has ever done before!

Kelvin is helped by having particularly elastic skin, and each challenge takes him around 15 minutes to complete. He usually adopts the same pattern when placing the pegs because at some point he knows he will be unable to see anything due to the number of clothespins. He starts under his ear and follows the jawline until he gets to his chin, then clips another row below that. Next he does the high cheekbone area and forehead. Last, he pins the areas around the eyes, nose, and mouth. He has to keep a straight face to avoid pegs falling off.

Despite the pain, Kelvin's ambition is to become the first person to clip thousands of clothes pegs onto his entire body.

▶ Kelvin really suffers for his art. "It hurts my skin and leaves marks on my face, like small contusions. It usually takes me one or two days to get better. That's why I don't practice often!"

RECORD-BREAKING

161 PEGS!!

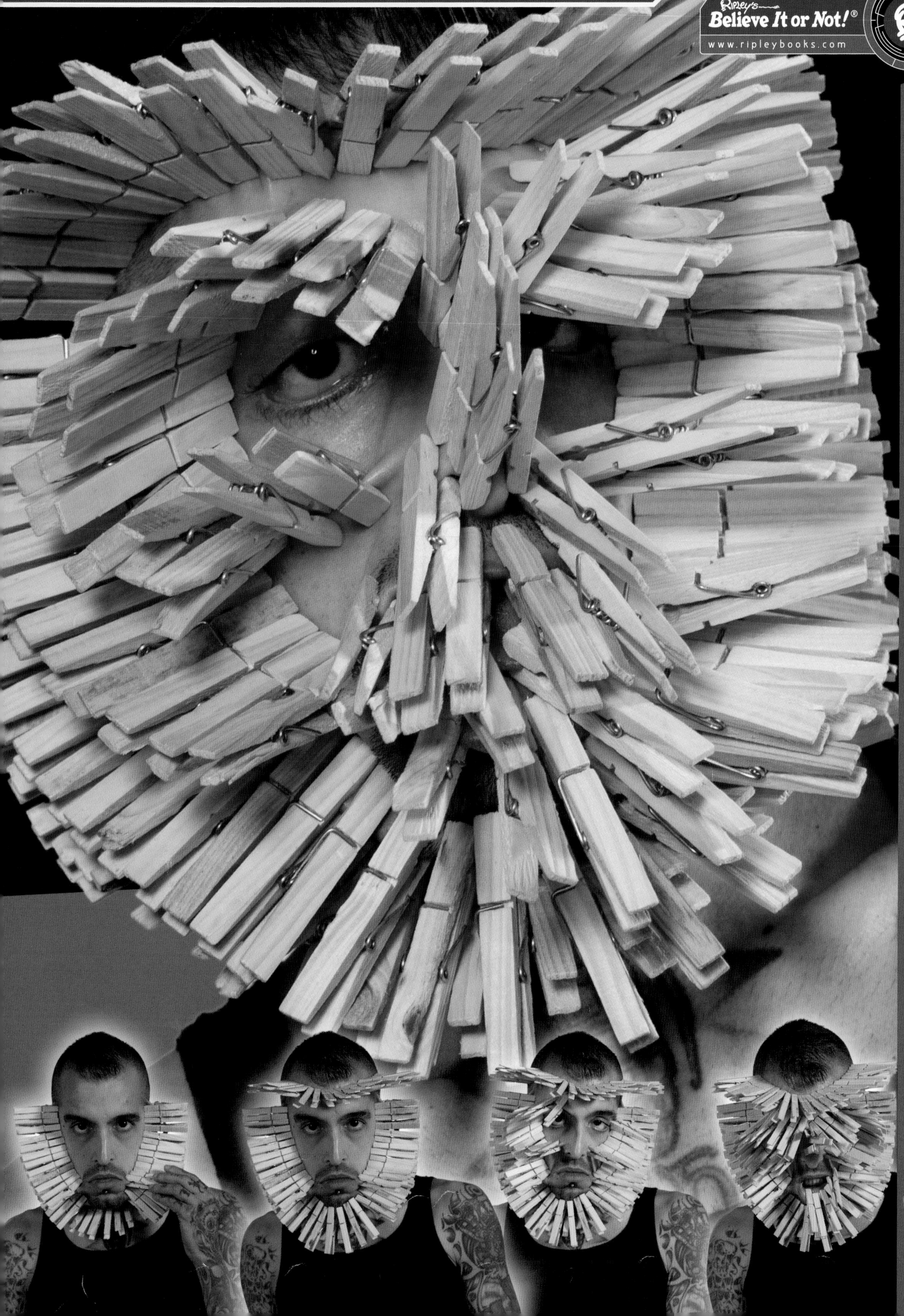

Rathakrishnan Velu

RAW STRENGTH

▶ **Kevin Shelley** of Carmel, Indiana, broke 46 wooden toilet seat lids in 60 seconds—with his head.

▶ **Steve Carrier** from Dallas, Texas, broke 30 baseball bats over his leg in under 60 seconds.

▶ **Kevin Taylor** of Clinton Township, Michigan, broke 584 cement bricks in 57.5 seconds with his hand.

▶ **Indian strongman Manoj Chopra** tore through fifty 2,000-page phone books in three minutes with his bare hands.

▶ **Larry Fields** of Kansas City, Kansas, smashed 354 cement patio blocks in one minute with his elbows.

▶ **Minoru Yoshida** of Japan once did 10,507 push-ups nonstop.

▶ **Rev. Les Davis** of Headland, Alabama, can bend steel bars in his teeth.

▶ **John Wooten** of West Palm Beach, Florida, has back-lifted a 7,000-lb (3,178-kg) elephant.

▶ **Iranian-German strongman Patrik Baboumian** can lift a 13-gal (50-l) beer keg weighing 330½ lb (150.2 kg)—that's around 15 lb (7 kg) heavier than he is—over his head.

BODY PULLING

▶ **Rathakrishnan Velu of Malaysia** (*above*) pulled a 327-ton train with his teeth.

▶ **Wang Ying of Jiangsu, China,** lifted 14 bricks with ropes attached to a 2-in-long (5-cm) tumor that had grown on his forehead.

▶ **Zhang Xingquan of Jilin, China,** pulled along a family car with his ear and while walking on raw eggs, none of which he broke during the feat.

▶ **Shailendra Roy of India** pulled a train engine and four coaches—a combined weight of over 44 tons—using only his hair, braided into a ponytail.

▶ **Ashok Verma of Agra, India,** lifted three 50-fl-oz (1.5-l) bottles of cola with a string attached to his eyelashes.

▶ **China's Fu Yingjie** pulled a 1.7-ton van and its driver more than 40 ft (12 m) with his nose.

▶ **Siba Prasad Mallick of Balasore, India,** pulled two motorcycles 1¼ mi (2 km) with his mustache.

QUICK OFF THE MARK

Paul Blair

▶ John Cassidy of Philadelphia, Pennsylvania, inflated and sculpted 747 balloons in one hour.

▶ Claude Breton picked 30,240 apples in eight hours at an orchard in Dunham, Quebec, Canada.

▶ Basketball-crazy Mike Campbell of Denver, Colorado, made 1,338 free throws in an hour—faster than one throw every three seconds—achieving a success rate of almost 90 percent.

▶ Garry Hebberman of Jamestown, Australia, sheared 1,054 sheep in 40 hours—that's one sheep every 2 minutes 17 seconds.

▶ Paul Blair (*right*) of San Francisco, California, can run a mile in under eight minutes while twirling a hula hoop.

▶ Germany's Christopher Irmscher completed the 100-meter hurdles in 14.82 seconds—while wearing swim fins on his feet.

▶ Ashrita Furman of New York City hopped a mile on one leg in 27 minutes 51 seconds.

▶ Jill Stamison of Grand Haven, Michigan, ran a 150-yard (137-m) sprint in 21.95 seconds while wearing 3-in (7.6-cm) high heels.

EXTREME JUGGLING

Milan Roskopf

▶ Kyle Petersen juggled three knives for 1 minute 2 seconds while riding a unicycle in New York City.

▶ With a single breath, Merlin Cadogan from Devon, England, juggled three objects underwater for 1 minute 20 seconds.

▶ Spain's Francisco Tebar Honrubia can juggle five Ping-Pong balls, using only his mouth and sending them up to 50 ft (15 m) in the air.

▶ Hanging from scaffolding and wearing special gravity boots, Erik Kloeker of Cincinnati, Ohio, juggled three balls upside down for over four minutes.

▶ Slovakia's Milan Roskopf (*left*) juggled three bowling balls, each weighing 12 lb (5 kg), for 28 seconds.

▶ While juggling chainsaws on July 28, 2008, Aaron Gregg of Victoria, Canada, achieved 88 catches.

▶ Australian performer Marty Coffey juggles an apple, a bowling ball, and an egg simultaneously, and during the stunt he even eats the apple.

▶ David Slick juggled three balls for 12 hours 5 minutes at North Richland Hills, Texas, in 2009.

MARATHON EFFORTS

▶ **Anthony Thornton walked backward for 24 hours around** Minneapolis, Minnesota, covering a distance of 95.7 mi (154 km).

▶ **Josef Resnik skied the same Austrian piste for 240 consecutive hours**—that's 10 days—taking only short breaks for the toilet and food.

▶ **Adrian Wigley from the West Midlands, England, played an electric organ nonstop for two hours—with his tongue.**

▶ **Tony Wright of Cornwall, England, stayed awake for over 11 days and nights** in 2007—a total of 266 hours.

▶ **India's Jayasimha Ravirala delivered a speech lasting 111 hours.**

▶ **Joseph Odhiambo dribbled a basketball through the streets of Houston, Texas, for 26 hours 40 minutes, during which time he bounced the ball** an estimated 140,000 times.

▶ **Rafael Mittenzwei roller-skated backward for over 129½ mi (208.4 km) in 24 hours around a track in Germany, completing 685 laps.**

MOUNTAIN SKATER

▶ Wearing his special 31-wheel roller suit, Jean-Yves skated down a Chinese mountain road containing 99 hairpin bends at speeds of up to 70 mph (112 km/h). During his descent of the 6.7-mi-long (10.77-km) road on Tianmen Mountain, he even completed a series of jumps over pits of sharp spikes.

Ripley's RESEARCH

French daredevil Jean-Yves Blondeau built his incredible Buggy Rollin' suit in 1995 as part of his graduation project at a Paris industrial design school. His aim was to create a wearable speed machine that would enable the human body to move freely in every direction. The body armor suit is equipped with 31 skateboard wheels on the torso, back, and most joints, allowing him to ride in every conceivable position—upright, on hands and knees, lying back luge-style, or racing downhill face-first with his nose 4 in (10 cm) from the ground. He can now reach 70 mph (112 km/h) and leap over 18½ ft (5.7 m) while wearing his suit.

YOUNG SCIENTIST ▶ At 17, Taylor Wilson of Reno, Nevada, was asked to advise the U.S. Department of Energy on nuclear fusion research, making him the world's youngest nuclear scientist. He has also built a functioning device that can detect nuclear weapons smuggled by would-be terrorists in cargo containers. At age seven, he had memorized every rocket made by the U.S. and Soviet governments from the 1930s onward, and by 14 he had built his own nuclear fusion reactor.

TIGER SUIT ▶ Wearing a 9-ft (2.7-m), 28-lb (13-kg) model tiger strapped to his back, Paul Goldstein from London, England, ran the Brighton and London marathons and climbed Africa's highest mountain, Kilimanjaro—all in eight days.

CANYON RIDE ▶ Sideshow performer Dextre Tripp from Minneapolis, Minnesota, entertains tourists by unicycling around the rim of the Grand Canyon above a 6,000-ft (1,800-m) vertical drop. As part of his act, the versatile artist can also walk uphill along a flaming tightrope 20 ft (6 m) in the air, juggle burning torches while standing on a person's shoulders, and slice an apple in his mouth with a chainsaw inches from his face.

BACKWARD SPELLER ▶ Shishir Hathwar of Bangalore, India, can spell 30 randomly chosen words backward in one minute. He can also pronounce words backward and can even spell the longest word in the Oxford English Dictionary—the 45-letter "pneumonoultramicroscopicsilicovolcanokoniosis" (a lung disease)—forward and backward.

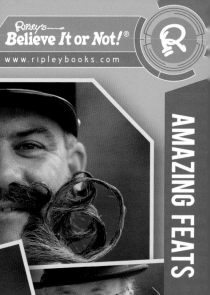

WACKY WHISKERS

▶ More than 150 competitors exhibited their carefully crafted facial hair at the 2012 European Beard and Mustache Championships in Wittersdorf, France. There were 18 different categories, including "Imperial Mustaches," "Dali Mustaches," and "Chin Beard Freestyle."

TIME TEAM▶ Roy and Pauline West have collected clocks for over 25 years and now have more than 4,000 crammed into their apartment near Southampton, England. The clocks cover every wall in their two-bedroom home—including 60 in the bathroom—and when the clocks change for British Summer Time, it takes the couple three days to reset them all.

TOY ARMY▶ The Museo de los Soldaditos de Plomo in Valencia, Spain, displays a collection of more than 85,000 toy soldiers and miniature figures—and keeps a million more in storage. The collection was started in 1941 when museum director Alejandro Noguera's father received a set of toy soldiers for his second birthday.

HUMAN DOMINOES▶ In just under ten minutes, 1,001 people were knocked backward in sequence onto mattresses in Shanghai, China, in July 2012 in an enormous chain of human dominoes.

FIGHTING FIT▶ In 2012, at the age of 73, boxing grandfather Paul N. Soucy of Livonia, Michigan, became a four-time Ringside World Champion—an incredible feat considering he has undergone heart bypass surgery, has metal plates in his ankle and neck, and is diabetic. Paul, who has been boxing since he was 19, won his age group in the 165-lb (75-kg) weight class at Kansas City, Missouri, by defeating Bill Cruze, also 73, in the third round. He had previously won the title in 2005, 2006, and 2008.

OLDEST SIBLINGS▶ In June 2012, 108-year-old Dorothy Richards and her sister, 105-year-old Marjorie Ruddle, became the world's oldest siblings. The sisters, who were raised in Northampton, England, clocked up a combined total of 213 years.

SPEEDY WHEELIE▶ A professional stunt rider for more than ten years, Ian Drummond, from Tyne and Wear, England, performed a 330-ft (100-m) bicycle wheelie in the lightning fast time of 13.7 seconds on August 27, 2012.

TEDDY TREASURE▶ The town of Hill City, South Dakota, has more teddy bears than human residents. That's because one of the 1,000 people living there is Jackie Miley who has a collection of over 7,800 teddies. Her house is filled from top to bottom with all types of bears, including Beanie Babies, Care Bears, and porcelain teddies.

While snowboarding on an icy glacier in Methven, New Zealand, Canada's Mark Sollors teetered on top of a natural quarter-pipe with a massive 40-ft (12-m) drop just inches ahead of him. Glacier snowboarders must also keep watch for dangerous holes in the ice that blend into the scenery. This spot was so inaccessible that Sollors had to be dropped there by helicopter.

Jumping from heights of up to 600 ft (183 m) without parachutes, extreme skiers plummet through the air at around 125 mph (200 km/h), yet they usually escape serious injury because they land in thick, soft snow. The snow cushions their fall, and that is why free skiers make their jumps in locations that always have plenty of fresh powder—such as Utah's Alta Ski Resort, which has an incredible 500 in (1,270 cm) of snowfall a year.

Julian Carr launches into a trademark flip off a 60-ft-high (18-m) cliff at Utah's Alta Ski Resort.

EXTREME SKIING

After months of planning, photographer Patrik Lindqvist captures Tomas Bergemalm's stunning leap from a 600-ft-high (183-m) French mountain cliff.

Female extreme skier Elyse Saugstad from Girdwood, Alaska, skis down a 20-ft (6-m) cliff covered in fresh snow at Washington's Mount Baker Ski Area on a day when there was an "insane" risk of avalanche.

Extreme skiing takes this winter sport to the max, with competitors defying the ever-present threat of deadly avalanches to ski or leap hundreds of feet down vertical mountain cliffs. Not content with simply jumping into the snowy abyss below, many extreme skiers perform daring twists and flips in midair during their fall.

When the late Jamie Pierre made a 255-ft (78-m) free-fall cliff drop—known as a huck—in Wyoming in 2006, without a helmet or parachute, he landed headfirst, creating a 10-ft (3-m) crater in the deep snow. Amazingly, his only injury was a cut lip—from the shovel his friends were using to dig him out of the hole!

That record height was more than doubled in 2011 by Swedish free skier Tomas Bergemalm, who jumped off a 600-ft-high (183-m) mountain cliff face near Chamonix, France, and landed safely—an incredible leap of faith that required five months of training. Thirty-five-year-old Tomas, who once skied across Greenland in just 47 days and has competed in ski competitions all over the world from Slovenia to Canada, wanted to make one last spectacular jump before retiring from the sport to spend more time with his family.

To record the jump—twice the height of the Statue of Liberty from ground to torch—Tomas teamed up with professional sports photographer Patrik Lindqvist. The thrill was as great for the photographer as the skier. Patrik loves his job so much, he says: "If I have to climb mountains and sleep overnight in a tent at minus 20 degrees, then so be it."

Another extreme skier who risks life and limb in pursuit of the ultimate adrenalin rush is Julian Carr from Salt Lake City, Utah. He regularly launches himself off cliffs, and in 2006 set a new world record by performing a front flip off a 210-ft-high (64-m) cliff in Switzerland.

TRIATHLON JUGGLER ▶

BATHTUB PADDLE ▶ Rob Knott from Somerset, England, paddled down the River Avon from Bath to Bristol in a bathtub, covering the 17 mi (27 km) in 13 hours 45 minutes.

FULL HOUSE ▶ Lawrence Cobbold has more than 20,000 bird ornaments in his home in Devon, England. He has been acquiring them for over 25 years, and his collection is now so big that he has to go to his parents' house for meals and to store his clothes because there is no room at his own home.

PENNY PYRAMID ▶ Tom Haffey of Denver, Colorado, used 626,780 pennies to build a pyramid weighing about 4,000 lb (1,814 kg).

MOUNTAIN KING ▶ Since 1989, when he was 29 years old, Nepalese climber Apa Sherpa has reached the summit of the world's highest mountain, Mount Everest, 21 times.

ROBOT RACER ▶ A four-legged robot called Cheetah set a new land speed record for legged robots on March 5, 2012, by running at 18 mph (29 km/h) on a treadmill at a laboratory in Massachusetts. The robot, designed by robotics specialists Boston Dynamics, mimics the running pattern of a real cheetah, stretching out and increasing its speed by flexing and unflexing its back with each stride.

OLDEST BARTENDER ▶ In April 2012, 97-year-old Angie MacLean became the world's oldest bartender when she celebrated nearly 20 years behind the bar at Panama Joe's Café in Bridgeport, Connecticut.

FREQUENT FLYER ▶ Tom Stuker, a sales consultant from Bloomingdale, Illinois, has collected ten million airline frequent-flyer miles. He has made over 6,000 flights in the past 30 years, clocking up enough air miles to have flown to the Moon and back 20 times. United Airlines has even named an airplane in his honor.

HEAD FOR NUMBERS ▶ On December 8, 2011, China's Wang Feng accurately recited a 500-digit number after memorizing it for just five minutes at the World Memory Championships in Guangzhou.

CAR CRAZY ▶ Charlie Mallon of Downingtown, Pennsylvania, has more than 2,100 items of Chevrolet memorabilia acquired over 40 years, including signs, racing flags, soda cans, books, hats, belts, shirts, miniature cars, drinking glasses, and playing cards.

UNDERWATER MARATHON ▶ Running on an underwater treadmill in a pool at Salem, Oregon, on September 9, 2012, Mike Studer completed a 26.2-mile (42-km) underwater marathon in 3 hours 44 minutes 52 seconds.

CONCERT IN THE CLOUDS

▶ Musician Oz Bayldon from London, England, staged a concert up in the clouds when he led a group to perform a 40-minute gig in freezing temperatures at an altitude of 21,825 ft (6,654 m) on the summit of Mera Peak in the Himalayas. The band trekked up the mountain carrying three guitars, an iPad, and a battery-powered speaker before performing to an audience of 14 that included fellow mountaineers.

▶ Joe Salter of Pensacola, Florida, completed a triathlon—while juggling balls the whole way. He swam 0.25 mi (0.4 km) backstroke while juggling three balls, cycled 16.2 mi (26 km) juggling two balls in one hand, and ran 4 mi (6.4 km) also while juggling—and still finished the event in under two hours, beating 99 non-juggling competitors. He completed the last two sections without dropping a ball, making more than 15,000 successful catches. A pioneer of joggling (juggling and running), Joe is the first person to be able to swim and juggle proficiently. He says: "I came up with the techniques. I wanted to achieve the goal of juggling a triathlon because it was unexplored territory. Swimming was the hardest part because I had to swim just using my legs. Cycling was also quite a challenge. I was going about 17 mph (27 km/h), was surrounded by other competitors, and had to toss the balls from one hand to the other when it was time to switch gears."

DISABLED DIVER

▶ Despite having no arms and no legs, French athlete Philippe Croizon became the first disabled person to dive to a depth of 108 ft (33 m) when he achieved the feat in a special diving pool in Brussels, Belgium, on January 10, 2013. When he swims, Philippe (left), who had his arms and legs amputated following a 20,000-volt electric-shock accident in 1994, uses specially adapted prosthetic limbs that have fins attached.

OTHER ACHIEVEMENTS

■ In 2010, Philippe became the first quadruple amputee to swim across the English Channel, between England and France, covering the 21 mi (34 km) in less than 14 hours.

■ During 2012, Philippe swam four inter-continental straits—Oceania to Asia (Papua New Guinea to Indonesia), Africa to Asia (Egypt to Jordan), Europe to Africa (Spain to Morocco), and North America to Asia (Alaska to Russia)—a total of 35.6 mi (57.3 km).

FALL GUYS

▶ *Daredevil kayakers Steve Fisher and Dale Jardine from South Africa, and Sam Drevo of the United States paddled up to the lip of the world's largest waterfall, the Victoria Falls, knowing that one slip would send them plunging more than 350 ft (106 m) to their death—no person has ever survived a fall into the raging torrents below. Also braving the crocodiles and hippos that lurk in the calmer waters at the top of the mile-wide falls between Zambia and Zimbabwe, they stood on one of the small rocky outcrops that appear at the edge of the falls in the dry season and peered over for the view of a lifetime.*

SOCCER BARBIE

▶ For her diploma in visual arts at Strasbourg, France, student Chloë Ruchon designed "Barbie Foot," a Barbie-themed table soccer game, where, instead of soccer players, two teams of fashion-conscious Barbie dolls spin their legs at the ball. The limited edition game went on sale in Paris for $12,000.

VERTICAL SPRINT▶

Attached to a safety rope, Belgian athlete Mark Sluszny completed a vertical run down the side of a 334-ft-high (102-m) building in Brussels in just 15.5 seconds.

MOTH MENACE▶ St. Louis Cardinals baseball player Matt Holliday exited a game against the L.A. Dodgers on August 22, 2011, in the eighth inning because he had a moth in his ear. Trainers had to pull the moth out using tweezers.

ACCIDENT PRONE▶ Since 1995, British racehorse jockey Robert "Choc" Thornton has suffered more than 360 falls and 40 serious injuries, including breaking all 24 ribs in his body, his right collarbone six times, and his left collarbone three times. He has also broken and lost several teeth.

SEVEN UP▶ A bet placed on 2012 Wimbledon men's singles tennis champion Roger Federer nine years earlier earned £100,000 ($160,000) for the charity Oxfam. In 2003, Nick Newlife from Oxfordshire, England, wagered £1,520 at odds of 66 to 1 that the Swiss player would win seven Wimbledon titles by 2019, a feat he achieved by defeating Scotland's Andy Murray seven years ahead of the expiry date. Mr. Newlife had died in 2009 but had left the betting slip to Oxfam in his will.

PILLOW FIGHT

▶ Hundreds of combatants attacked each other with pillows during a half-hour battle in Trafalgar Square, London, England, on April 7, 2012. As part of the Seventh Annual Pillow Fight Day, similar mass scuffles took place in more than 100 cities across the world, including Los Angeles, Sydney, Madrid, São Paulo, and Shanghai.

▸ **STRONG SKIN** Chinese kung fu performer Huang Yao, 63, can carry heavy objects—such as two buckets of water—suspended from needles inserted through the skin of his neck and arms. He can also swallow solid steel balls and stand barefoot on two razor-sharp knife blades. As a boy Yao was unable to walk until he was six or talk until he was eight, so to improve his education his parents sent him to the Wenshu Temple, where the monks also taught him to perform his eye-watering stunts.

GREAT ESCAPE▸ Daredevil Anthony Martin from Wisconsin freed himself from shackles and a locked casket while plummeting to the Earth at 130 mph (210 km/h). Anthony performed the amazing feat to celebrate the release of his new book: "Escape or Die An Escape Artist Unlocks The Secret To Cheating Death."

BIRTHDAY TO REMEMBER▸ To celebrate her 101st birthday, great-grandmother Mary Allen Hardison of Ogden, Utah, went paragliding. She made the flight because she was determined not to be outdone by her 75-year-old son Allen who had recently taken up paragliding.

SHARED NAMES▸ Alex Nunn of Ipswich, England, spent more than ten years visiting seven other places around the world also called Ipswich. His 61,000-mi (98,000-km) odyssey took him to Ipswiches in Massachusetts, South Dakota, New Hampshire, Jamaica, Queensland (Australia), and Manitoba (Canada), plus Ipswitch, Wisconsin.

NUN PARADE▸ In June 2012, 1,436 men and women dressed as nuns and paraded through the town of Listowel, County Kerry, Ireland.

BUSY BUS▸ On April 20, 2012, a total of 246 students from a school in Kielce, Poland, squeezed into a single-decker city bus, setting a new world record for the most people crammed in a bus.

JAW DROPPING!▸ Martial arts teacher Dragon Jetlee broke 150 eggs with his chin—one egg at a time—in 60 seconds in Tiruchirappalli, India.

SPEED SKIPPER▸ Army Major Leticia Walpole jumped rope 9,335 times in an hour at Fort Leavenworth, Kansas, on May 10, 2012—that amounts to 155 jumps per minute, or 2½ per second!

OLDEST CLIMBER▸ Following a six-day trek, 84-year-old Richard Byerley from Walla Walla, Washington State, became the oldest person to climb the 19,340-ft-high (5,895-m) Mount Kilimanjaro in Tanzania on foot. He reached the summit on October 6, 2011, with his two grandchildren, Annie, 29, and Bren, 25.

AUTO FLIP ▸ Aaron Evans of Milwaukee, Wisconsin, does death-defying somersaults over cars that are moving at speeds of 30 mph (48 km/h). Inspired to take up gymnastics after watching a Bruce Lee movie when he was five, he tackles the cars head on. He takes a short run-up, leaps into the air a split second before the front bumper is about to hit him, then performs a full flip in midair and lands well behind the car. In 2011, he jumped over three moving cars in just over a minute.

Pinned through the skin!

GIANT SKATEBOARD▶ A team of six U.K. engineers took 300 hours to build a giant skateboard measuring 22 ft (6.7 m) long, 8 ft (2.4 m) wide, and weighing 560 lb (254 kg)—big enough to hold 30 children at once and weighing as much as a baby African elephant.

CARD SHARP▶ Ye Tongxin from Nanjing, China, can slice 12 cucumbers in 47 seconds by throwing playing cards at them ninja-style.

RUBIK ROBOT▶ A robot made out of LEGO® blocks and powered by an Android smartphone has broken the record for the fastest time to solve a Rubik's Cube. In London, England, on November 11, 2011, CubeStormer II, invented by David Gilday and Mike Dobson, solved the puzzle in just 5.27 seconds—faster than any human. The robot uses a cell-phone camera to take images of each face of the Rubik's Cube, then analyzes the images and sends instructions via Bluetooth to four LEGO arms, which rotate the cube at high speed.

POLE SKI▶ In December 2011, 16-year-old Amelia Hempleman-Adams, daughter of British adventurer David Hempleman-Adams, became the youngest person to ski to the South Pole. She skied 97 mi (156 km) to the Pole and she and her father spent 17 nights on the ice, enduring sub-zero temperatures, whiteouts, and 24-hour daylight.

GLACIER PLUNGE▶ Californian thrill-seeker Ben Stookesberry became the first person to kayak down a glacial waterfall when he plunged over the 65-ft-high (20-m) Braswell Glacier in Svalbard, Arctic Circle, and into the icy waters below.

WALKING DEAD

▶ Nearly 10,000 people wearing ghoulish makeup and ragged clothes splattered with fake blood shambled in a trance-like state through the streets of Mexico City on November 26, 2011, in what was the world's biggest zombie walk. Since the first recognized zombie parade was staged in Sacramento, California, in 2001, similar walks have taken place all over the world—including in Australia, Canada, and Argentina.

INDEX

ACKNOWLEDGMENTS

Cover (l) Anthony Martin Skydive Chicago; **4** Caters News; **6–7** Caters News; **8** (t) Caters News, (b) Shareef Sarhan; **9** Quirky China News/Rex Features; **10** Jay Nemeth/Red Bull Content Pool; **11** (b/r) balazsgardi.com/Red Bull Content Pool, (t/r) Joerg Mitter/Red Bull Content Pool, (b/l) Red Bull Stratos/Red Bull Content Pool; **12** (t/l, r) Getty Images, (b) L.L.Bean/Rex Features; **13** Getty Images; **14** (t) Top Photo Corporation/Rex Features, (b) Reuters/Vladimir Nikolsky; **15** Canadian Press/Rex Features; **16–17** Alexander Remnev/Solent News/Rex Features; **17** Helma van der Weide/Rex Features; **18** (t) WENN.com, (b) Getty Images; **19** Caters News; **22** (t) Vincent Thian/AP/Press Association Images, (b) Getty Images; **23** Reuters/Laszlo Balogh; **24** Imaginechina/Rex Features; **25** Reuters/Vincent Kessler; **26** (l) Caters News, (r) Scott Markewitz; **27** (b/l) Grant Gunderson, (l) Caters News, (t/r) Alaska Stock Images/National Geographic Stock; **28** (t/l, t/c) Joe Salter, Flora Bama-Lounge Triathlon, (t/r) Jeff Nelson Studios, (b) Gennaro Serra; **29** (c, t/l) Jeff Nelson Studios, (t/r) Joe Salter, Flora Bama-Lounge Triathlon, (b) Reuters/Yves Herman; **30** Desre Pickers; **31** (t, r) NTI Media Ltd/Rex Features, (b) © Ian Marlow/Demotix/Corbis; **32** (t) Anthony Martin Skydive Chicago, (b) Quirky China News/Rex Features; **33** AFP/Getty Images; **Back cover** Gennaro Serra

Key: t = top, b = bottom, c = center, l = left, r = right, sp = single page, dp = double page

All other photos are from Ripley Entertainment Inc.
Every attempt has been made to acknowledge correctly and contact copyright holders and we apologize in advance for any unintentional errors or omissions, which will be corrected in future editions.